Star Bird

Kylee Dylan

BookLeaf Publishing

India | USA | UK

Presentation by *BookLeaf Publishing*

Web: www.bookleafpub.com

E-mail: info@bookleafpub.com

ISBN: 9789363309616

First edition 2024

To all those I've loved. To those who broke my heart. And to those who live in between.

We're All Dying

I have never been afraid of death
It is an inescapable fate
A cold hard fact
I've always been more afraid of life
And the things that make you feel dead
Many people die long before they actually pass
away
They die a little everyday
One heart break at a time

Hurt

2

I didn't need you to hurt me
I can hurt myself better than anyone
I can make every pump of blood in my body
feel like a storm
Rattling chaos and weaponizing every bit of love
you never gave me

Fairytale Lies

We're fed fairytale lies from birth
We're taught love will always win
That a kiss can cure all
But sometimes hearts do break
and we bleed misery
We cry and ache
and no amount of tears
can drown the pain

Self Reflection

My heart broke
when you pretended to love me
But my heart shattered
when I pretended to love myself
I force-fed my self sabotage
and starved myself of worth
I couldn't even pretend
to give a damn

Time

5

All I wanted was time
Time is the world's most precious currency
It can be given
It can be wasted
It can be shared
But it cannot go back
We can only move forward
And if you're not busy living
Then you're busy dying
It's only a matter of time

I Promise

6

One day
We will be somewhere
You will be You
And I will be Me
We will be together there
It will be perfect
I promise.

Walls

I thought I'd be better
I thought I'd be stronger
I said 'yes'
When I should have screamed 'no'
I abandoned the people I loved
And kept those that only took for themselves
I built walls around me to protect you
But they just weren't tall enough

Would You?

8

If I could
Take all your pain
I would
If I could
Fix everything
I would
If I could
Promise that nothing
Would ever hurt you again
Would you let me?

Purpose

My purpose is to let you know that you're loved
And to tell you that you're a beautiful soul
And that this world is so lucky to have you
I will remind you everyday
Whether you want to hear it or not

Never Again

I know what it is like to lose
I have lost everything
More than I can count
I had to learn how to live again
I had to learn how to love at all
I had to build myself up
So strongly that I couldn't fall
I will not lose again
Never again

The Price of Love

I never knew love
That didn't come at a price
So when it was given to me
I didn't recognize
Years of being numb
And hoping for the best
Felt far too heavy
Weighing on my chest
The guilt overtakes me
And every time I cry
I lost you long before
We ever said goodbye

The Storm

I survived the storm
That took so many
When I see
all those that lost
I wonder why?
Surely, I was just as good
and just as bad as they were
They had plans-didn't they?
They wanted more-right?
I wish I could've saved them
They call them lost
But so was I
Yet somehow, I survived

Star Bird

I never felt like a flower
I wasn't a delicate rose
I was wild from the start
A lone wolf
Trying to find my way
A rebel
Looking for a cause
A delinquent
Defying the odds
I tried to destroy myself
a million different ways
Before I realized
that I wasn't the enemy
I am strong
I am resilient
a star bird

I Can Only Hope

It used to be
That I would wake up
Every morning and he was there
I would grab him tightly in bed
and kiss him good morning
We would drink coffee
and talk about our day
It never occurred to me
that it wouldn't last forever
These days
I wake up alone
I lay in bed
I drink coffee
and think about the day
I miss the way it was
All I can hope is
One day
I'll wake up
and he'll be there
We'll drink coffee
and lay in bed all day
and it will be like no time has passed

Past-Passed

15

You can judge me
for a lot of things
But don't judge me for my past
I have done so much
and worked so hard
to get as far away from there as possible
That isn't me anymore
and never will be again
I had to live in a prison
that was locked from inside
I've seen days so dark
they look like midnight
I planned my own funeral
Before I planned my escape
It took a long time
But the wait was worth it

Memory

I hate it when
I want to hate you
I try to be angry
and I picture
your big dumb brown eyes
and I feel myself smile
I remember how
I would stroke your hair in bed
and hold your hand in the car
and my eyes get wet
I can't hate you
because you are
still so important to me
Even if only in memory

Strangers

It's crazy the way
Someone can be a complete stranger to you
When at one time
You knew them
Inside and out
Now everything about them
Is a mystery
and you wonder
How life can be so cruel
And time can be so harsh

Beautiful, Golden, Misery

18

To know you was beautiful
To have loved you was golden
To have lost you was complete and utter misery

I Miss You

I miss you
I know its been a long time
and I know we haven't spoken
but after all this time
I still have moments when I wish you were here
I'll hear a funny joke and want to tell you
Or I'll hear a great song and want to show you
I'll go to call you and remember I can't
I always have an empty place
next to me where you should be
no one will ever replace you

The Middle

I can't remember
the last time I was truly happy
I mean one of those moments
when you feel complete
I am not unhappy
I just am
It is a weird purgatory
it's not quite misery
but it's not quite happiness either
I know something is missing
when I find it
I will know
until then I'm stuck in the middle
doing the best I can

Ordinary

I don't mind ordinary
Some of the best things
in life are ordinary
The little moments
and mundane memories
End up being the big things
you remember later

www.ingramcontent.com/pod-product-compliance
Lightning Source LLC
LaVergne TN
LVHW050307200726

843509LV00015B/3212